Texas

BY HOLLY SAARI

The Child's World

Published by The Child's World®
1980 Lookout Drive • Mankato, MN 56003-1705
800-599-READ • www.childsworld.com

ACKNOWLEDGMENTS
The Child's World®: Mary Berendes, Publishing Director
The Design Lab: Design and production
Red Line Editorial: Editorial direction

PHOTO CREDITS: Alexey Stiop/iStockphoto, cover, 1, 3; Matt Kania/Map
Hero, Inc., 4, 5; John Zellmer/iStockphoto, 7; Eric Foltz/iStockphoto, 9;
iStockphoto, 10; Dave Huss/iStockphoto, 11; Dale Woodall/Bigstock, 13;
North Wind Picture Archives/Photolibrary, 15; Chad Breece/iStockphoto, 17;
Chris Pizzello/AP Images, 19; Steve Vidler/Photolibrary, 21; One Mile Up,
22; Quarter-dollar coin image from the United States Mint, 22

LIBRARY OF CONGRESS CATALOGING-IN-PUBLICATION DATA
Saari, Holly.
  Texas / by Holly Saari.
      p. cm.
  Includes bibliographical references and index.
  ISBN 978-1-60253-488-9 (library bound : alk. paper)
  1. Texas—Juvenile literature. I. Title.

F386.3.S23 2010
976.4—dc22

                            2010018409

Printed in the United States of America in Mankato, Minnesota.
July 2010
F11538

On the cover:
The Alamo in
San Antonio,
Texas, is one of
the state's most
famous places.

CONTENTS

Geography

Let's explore Texas! Texas is in the southern United States. It is next to the **Gulf** of Mexico. Texas shares its southwestern border with Mexico. Texas is the second-largest state after Alaska.

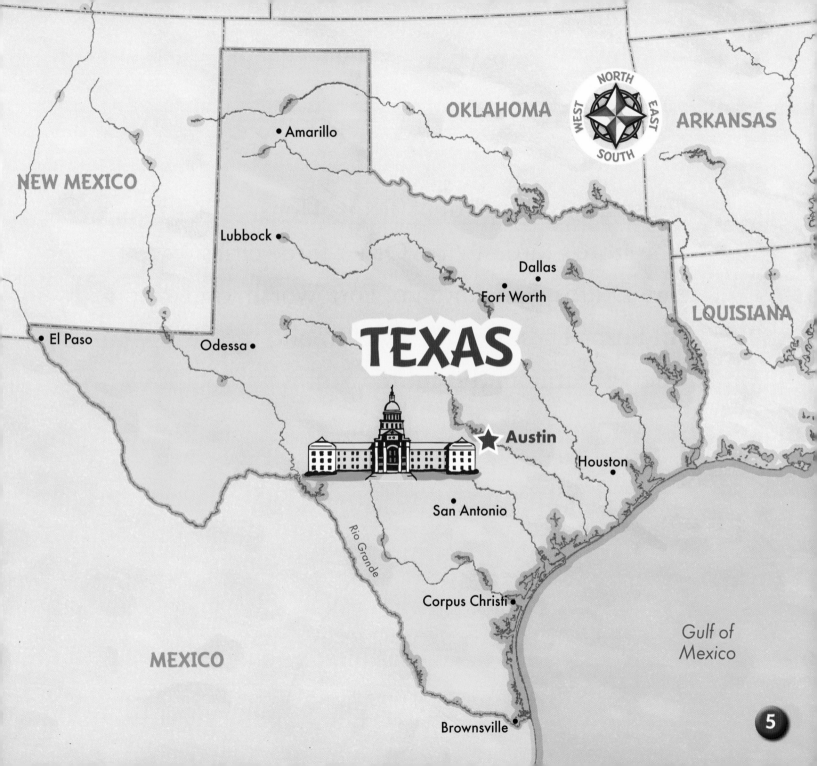

NEW MEXICO

OKLAHOMA

ARKANSAS

NORTH
WEST · EAST
SOUTH

Amarillo

Lubbock

Dallas
Fort Worth

LOUISIANA

El Paso

Odessa

TEXAS

Austin

Houston

San Antonio

Rio Grande

Corpus Christi

MEXICO

Gulf of
Mexico

Brownsville

Cities

Austin is the capital of Texas. Houston is the state's largest city. Other large cities are Dallas, San Antonio, Fort Worth, and El Paso. These six cities are among the 25 biggest cities in the United States.

Houston is home to more than 2.1 million people. ▶

Land

Texas has **plains**, hills, forests, and beaches. The Rio Grande is a river that runs through the state. It also forms the southwestern border of the state. Texas has a lot of oil underground.

The Rio Grande separates Texas from Mexico. ▶

Plants and Animals

Deer, armadillos, coyotes, and lizards live in Texas. The state bird is the mockingbird. It can copy the sounds of other birds. Texas has many types of grasses and wildflowers. The state flower is the bluebonnet. It has small blue **petals**. Crabs and shrimp live in the coastal waters along the Gulf of Mexico.

Beautiful bluebonnets are a source of pride for Texans. ▶

People and Work

More than 24 million people live in Texas. Only California has more people. Most Texans live in cities. Many people work in jobs that deal with oil. Some people make machines, food, and **chemicals**. Some people raise cattle.

Many cattle are raised in central and western Texas. ▶

History

Native Americans have lived in this area for thousands of years. People from Spain began exploring the area in the 1500s. Spain, France, and Mexico have each owned the area at different times. U.S. settlers moved to the area in the 1800s. Texas became the twenty-eighth state on December 29, 1845.

Texas was its own nation from 1836 to 1845. It was called the Republic of Texas.

San Antonio is a historic city in Texas. ▶

Ways of Life

Texas's history as a **frontier** is important in the state. Texas is well known for **cowboys** who explored the area on horseback while raising cattle. Sports are very **popular** in Texas, especially football. The state has many **professional** sports teams.

Many Texans enjoy going to **rodeos**. ▶

Famous People

Former U.S. President Lyndon Johnson was born in Texas. Singers Beyoncé Knowles and Hilary Duff were born here, too.

Former U.S. President George W. Bush grew up in Texas. He later became governor of the state.

Hilary Duff starred as "Lizzie McGuire" on the Disney Channel show of the same name. ▶

Famous Places

The Alamo is in San Antonio. Texas and Mexico fought an important battle here. The Alamo is a popular place to visit. Houston is home to the Johnson Space Center. People working here study the solar system and discover things in space.

Visitors to the Johnson Space Center can see space rockets. ▶

21

State Symbols

Seal

The state seal of Texas has two tree branches. One stands for strength. The other stands for peace. Texas's state seal has two sides. Go to childsworld.com/links for a link to Texas's state Web site, where you can get a firsthand look at the state seal.

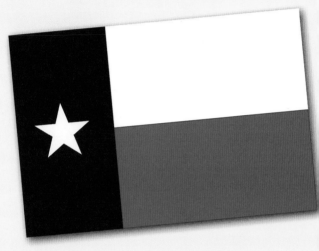

Flag

Texas is known as "the Lone Star State." This is because it had been an **independent** republic. Texas only has one star on its flag to show that it stood alone.

Quarter

Texas's state quarter has a star and a **lariat** to represent the state's history. The quarter came out in 2004.

Glossary

chemicals (KEM-uh-kulz): Chemicals are substances used in chemistry. Chemicals are made in Texas.

cowboys (KOW-boyz): Cowboys are men who take care of cattle or horses. Many cowboys explored the Texas area.

frontier (frun-TEER): A frontier is the edge of an area that has not yet been explored. Texas was part of the American frontier.

gulf (GULF): A gulf is a large body of water with land around most of it. Texas is next to the Gulf of Mexico.

independent (in-deh-PEN-dent): If an area is independent, it rules itself. Texas was once independent.

lariat (LAYR-ee-ut): A lariat is a long piece of rope with a loop at one end to catch an animal. A lariat appears on the Texas state quarter.

petals (PET-ulz): Petals are the colorful parts of flowers. Texas's state flower, the bluebonnet, has blue petals.

plains (PLAYNZ): Plains are areas of flat land that do not have many trees. Texas has plains.

popular (POP-yuh-lur): To be popular is to be enjoyed by many people. Sports are popular in Texas.

professional (pro-FESH-uh-nul): Professional means getting paid to do something that others do only for fun. Texas has many professional sports teams.

republic (ri-PUB-lik): A republic is a type of government in which people elect representatives who make laws. Texas was once its own republic.

rodeos (ROH-dee-ohz): Rodeos are contests in which people ride horses and rope cattle. Rodeos are popular in Texas.

seal (SEEL): A seal is a symbol a state uses for government business. Texas's seal shows branches to stand for strength and peace.

symbols (SIM-bulz): Symbols are pictures or things that stand for something else. The seal and the flag are Texas's symbols.

Further Information

Books

Crane, Carol. *L is for Lone Star: A Texas Alphabet*. Chelsea, MI: Sleeping Bear Press, 2001.

Keller, Laurie. *The Scrambled States of America*. New York: Henry Holt, 2002.

Sasek, M. *This is Texas*. New York: Universe Publishing, 2006.

Web Sites

Visit our Web site for links about Texas: *childsworld.com/links*

Note to Parents, Teachers, and Librarians: We routinely verify our Web links to make sure they are safe and active sites. So encourage your readers to check them out!

Index